A Voice in the Wilderness
vol.2

THE EARLY YEARS

by

Dr. Dalen Garris

DALEN GARRIS

This is a work of history. Historical individuals and places and events are mentioned.

Copyright © 2020 by Dr. Dalen Garris

Published by Revivalfire Ministries
Cover Design by Kevin Haislip
Cover picture by Chris Barbalis

ISBN 13: 978-1-7342213-1-2
ISBN 10: 1-7342213-1-3

All rights reserved.
No part of this book may be used or reproduced in any manner whatsoever, without written permission, except in the case of brief quotations embodied in critical articles and reviews, as provided by U.S. Copyright Law.

For information, address
dale@revivalfire.org

First paperback printing November 2020

Printed in the United States of America

Table of Contents

Preface	1
Choices	3
The Need for Recognition	5
How Do You Define a Christian?	7
Legalism	9
Heroes	12
In A Word	14
Perspective	16
Lamentations Coming	18
The Bride	20
The Waters of Marah	22
And He Could There Do No Mighty Work	24
Dumb Peter	27
Stand	29
THE NEW SCHOOL PRAYER	31
The Alabaster Box	33
A Father's Agonizing Decision	35
Ol' Blind Bartimaeus	37
The Gospel According to Rene Descartes	39
The Cycle of Apostasy	41
The Emperor's Clothes	43
Hector, the Soul Collector	46
Prophets	48
The Making of a Prophet	51
Famine	52
Mahershalalhasbaz	54

Hatred	57
A Touch From the Finger of God.	59
Worship	61
Hem of His Garment	64
Leaves of Grass	66
The Toy Store	68
New Things	71
Broken Hearts	74
Preparation in Prayer	76
Two Simple Things	79
Gideon's Stand	81
Once Upon A Time…	84
I Remember When We Were Young	86
Brokenness	88
Rain	90
15 Minutes of Fame	92
Religious Spirit	94
The Death of Saul	96
About the Author	98
Books by Dalen Garris:	100

Preface

The theme of this series, "A Voice in the Wilderness", reflects the nature and call of articles that I wrote over the course of a decade. They were printed in several newspapers and emailed around the world in an attempt to call the Church out of the spiritual desert she was in, and see Her return to what she once was - a vibrant, on-fire fortress of righteousness and salvation to a lost and dying world.

I felt a call to make the crooked ways straight and prepare the way for the Coming of the Lord. How soon would that be? I have no idea, but I do know that the Lord often takes 20 to 40 years in preparation for a move of the Holy Spirit, so I started writing.

There is no order to these articles. They just came as they were given. I never knew when then next one would come, and I never knew what it would be about. Whenever the Lord would drop another message on me, the next few hours would belong to Him as the words poured out of me.

And that is what it is like – the words pour out onto the pages almost of their own volition. Sometimes I would start by lifting my palms up and ask for Him to anoint my fingers as I typed ... and He always did.

These articles are not mine. If I could I would put His name as the author, but that would sound tacky. Nevertheless, He and I both know that He wrote these articles, not me.

I hope that, as you read through them, you will realize that also.

==================================

The voice of him that crieth in the wilderness, Prepare ye the way of the LORD, make straight in the desert a highway for our God.

Every valley shall be exalted, and every mountain and hill shall be made low: and the crooked shall be made straight, and the rough places plain:

And the glory of the LORD shall be revealed, and all flesh shall see it together: for the mouth of the LORD hath spoken it.

(Isaiah 40:3-5)

Choices

"There but for the grace of God go I."

How many times have we repeated that timeworn phrase when looking at someone more unfortunate than ourselves? Sometimes it's financial troubles, sometimes personal problems; sometimes we have brought it upon ourselves and are just reaping for mistakes we have made. Sometimes the unexpected is simply thrust upon us for no earthly reason. We say it as a prayer of thankfulness to God that, somehow, we have been spared what we see happen to others.

"Life isn't always fair" and "bad things happen to good people" are another couple of sayings we repeat to explain things that we don't understand. Does God just pick at random those who will go through tough times and those who will not? Is it just a matter of chance? Or is there something more to it than meets the eye?

I believe that people make choices in life that steer them to destinations that they hadn't figured on. Little choices. Everyday decisions. Slight changes in attitude. Life is a long journey, and small directional changes can take us way off the originally intended path. Sometimes we end up in a certain place and wonder how we got so far off the course. Sometimes we end up satisfied with our own delusions and never realize how far off we are. Is it "but for the grace of God" that we don't end up like that, or was it a matter of little choices that made the difference?

I don't believe that Life is a Monopoly game that is dependent on the roll of the dice. We make choices in life that steer us to predictable results. All of us suffer through ups and downs, and we make the best of the challenges that we all have to face, but Life isn't measured by good fortune. It is measured by how we deal with the challenges we are presented with. If no one was ever sick, and no one ever had troubles, and there was no death, what kind of a world would we be living in? And how would the Lord be able to deal with us to bring us to a place where we will seek His face?

Do we win in Life because we ended up with all the toys? If that was the case, only the rich, beautiful, and lucky would go to heaven, and the rest of us would burn in Hell. Or is Life really just a dressing room for Eternity where we are tested to see if, in spite of everything, we will choose God? What is your main focus in Life? What is your primary goal? What is it that you are trying to attain to?

Little choices take us in different directions. I want to make sure that the choices I make are nested deep within the grace of God.

The Need for Recognition

An intrinsic part of human nature, to a varying degree, is the need to feel good about oneself. We would also like for others to think well of us and bolster that feeling of self-worth. We all know someone that, no matter what story you have, they have one better. It's called "one-up-man-ship," and it's really just an indication that this person has a strong need for some kind of personal recognition. They need to show you how good they are.

Pride is an invisible sin because you can't see it in yourself. It also takes many different forms. It is not just thinking you're better than others. Sometimes it takes the form of being afraid that you really aren't as good as others and wanting so desperately to feel good about yourself. This turns into a form of pride when you start to focus on yourself instead of others, and you start measuring yourself against everyone else. The result? You have to tell everyone how special you are with God.

In the ministry, this can take some dangerous turns. I am not impressed with all the great and supernatural things that somebody has done. Whenever I have run into people for whom everything is supernatural, they seem very impressive at first, but I have always ended up being disappointed with their lack of depth in God. I believe in the supernatural as much as or more than most people, but I have never seen the real warriors of God, those servants who really oozed with power and authority in God, running around to let everybody know how supernatural their walk with God was. Instead, they are usually focused on letting you know how powerful <u>your</u> walk in God could be. Funny how it's just the opposite.

Everybody has a certain need for recognition, true, but while some give themselves over to it, others deny it and give their lives over as a sacrifice to God to serve others. It's a matter of where your focus is in life. Either you are concerned with yourself and your standing with others, or you are concerned with others and their standing with God. One or the other.

Ephesians 5:1 tells us to be followers of God and walk in love, as Christ has loved us. Sounds great, doesn't it. But the rest of the scripture tells us what walking in love really means:

> *"...and hath given himself for us an offering and a sacrifice to God."*

Uh oh. There's that word again – "sacrifice", the exact antithesis of pride.

Recognize the needs in others, and God will take care of the needs in you. Deny thyself, crucify your flesh so you can walk in the Spirit of God, and He will not only give you power over sin, but also that overcoming feeling of Victory. Only He can give you that victory; you can't get it for yourself. And when you are walking in victory, you won't need the recognition of others.

Then and only then, can God start to use you in a powerful way.

How Do You Define a Christian?

How do you define a Christian? The Bible is pretty clear that, as the old song goes, "everybody that's talkin' 'bout Heaven ain't goin' there." There's some sheep, and there are some goats; there's wheat, and there are tares; there were those five virgins that were wise, and the five that were foolish. Where does one draw the line, and what is it that God is looking for?

If it were just a matter of going to a church, then just about everybody would be going to Heaven. But the Bible doesn't say that. As a matter of fact, it says that strait and narrow is the path that leads to Heaven, and few there be that find it.

How about belief? If you really believe that God is up there, doesn't that count? Well, I see that the children of Israel believed in God as they headed for the Promised Land. How could they not believe? They ate manna every day, drank water out of a rock, and followed a pillar of cloud by day and a pillar of fire by night. (If some of today's atheistic intellectuals had been there, I'm sure they'd come up with a fancy, complicated explanation for it that no one could understand. After all, look at their theories about Evolution.) Nevertheless, the Children of Israel knew it was God. And yet, the Bible says they entered not in because of unbelief.

How about all these souped-up, high-powered TV preachers? Sounds like they've got a good hold on Heaven. After all, look at all the cool stuff they can do. If you haven't heard about all the wonderful stuff they've done, just ask them. They'd love to tell you. But somehow, I don't think the Lord is all that impressed.

He's not impressed with our great and mighty deeds; He's impressed with the challenges we have met and have overcome. That, to me, is encouraging. It's not the mountain tops that you've been on that count with Him, but the valleys that you've gone through that give you your depth in God.

People that have sincere hearts before God, that desire Truth in the inward parts, are the ones that impress me. I think God is impressed with them also.

> *Suffer the little children to come unto me, and forbid them not: for of such is the kingdom of God. Verily I say unto you, Whosoever shall not receive the kingdom of God as a little child, he shall not enter therein. Mark 10:15*

Legalism

Legalism. Who was it that coined that word, anyway? I'm told that it refers to those who, like the Pharisees, relied upon their own righteous works to attain to the righteousness of God. Well, they're easy to pick on. They were prime targets for Jesus' parables, so there's little doubt about where they stand in the eyes of God. But I have yet to find anyone who seriously believes that we can keep all the commandments through the efforts of our flesh and our own willpower. And yet I hear this term thrown around all over the place. Who are these "legalists" that we are so ready to condemn? Or is this just another excuse to justify sin?

I've heard people point to preachers of righteousness, call them legalists, and condemn them as being too hard and exacting. Well, Noah was a preacher of righteousness, and the Bible says that he condemned the world. And here's the scary part, Jesus said that as it was in the days of Noah, so shall it be just before He returns. Human nature just doesn't change much, does it?

Then, on the other hand, we have the "Name it, and Claim it" crowd that believes that God owes us all the prosperity, money, power, wealth, and health that you can grab ahold of. All you have to do is claim it! If you are going through any adversity, it's because of a lack of faith. Well, tell that to Job. And what about the men and women in Hebrews chapter 11? Did they just not claim deliverance hard enough? Somebody needs to let God know because He thinks that they're heroes.

I've also noticed that the same crowd that condemns

Legalists is the same one that loves "prosperity" messages. "God is Love," they say, and He understands our shortcomings and will excuse us because He has unconditional Love. The so-called "Legalists", on the other hand, say that the love of God is shown by the keeping of His commandments. Who should we believe?

You can find the passages where God explains the whole purpose of the new covenant in Jeremiah and Ezekiel. Jesus didn't die just to pay the price for our sins. Neither did He die to give us an excuse to sin because we are now under Grace. That's not Grace. Jesus died to give us an opportunity to actually receive the Spirit of God into our hearts so that we would take on the very nature of God and have the power within us to overcome sin.

What an incredible offer! Repent of our old sins and receive Jesus Christ into our hearts as our personal Savior, and we can physically feel the weight of sin removed. We now have the power to be righteous before God! Not by our own works but by having Him work in us.

Ahhhh, but there's a catch here. You must choose to walk in Him daily. You have to walk in the Spirit of God in order to have the Spirit of God work in you.

Do you devour His Word as the Bread of Life that will sustain you? Or do you read it as if it was some textbook? Do you contend before the Throne of Grace for a move of God? Or do you pray little form prayers and hope that somebody up there will hear you? How deep are you walking in Him? That's how deep He's walking in you, and that's how much power you will have in God to overcome sin. There's not much room here for excuses because He's made it so simple and easy.

Thou wilt keep him in perfect peace, whose mind is stayed on thee: because he trusteth in thee. - Isaiah 26:3

Heroes

"And what shall I more say?" (Hebrews 11:32)

With these words, Paul winds up God's Honor Roll of saints who paid the price for a Gospel that they were willing to defend no matter what the outcome. These men and women left us an undying testimony of courage and faith that we can look to as evidence that there is something more to the Gospel than just another philosophy about God, Life, and Reality. They had a grip on something that they knew was more real than real, and they were willing to give their lives for it.

Wouldn't you love to meet them and see the fire of God burning in their eyes? They had something that fueled them to stand for something that this world no longer seems to value. Where can we go today to find that kind of victorious stand in the face of a society that is rushing headlong into sin, pleasure, and prosperity?

The Gospel they gave their lives for has never changed. Neither has the propensity of human flesh to seek after the things that appeal to the here and now. We may have a tendency to be enamored with the present – what we can see, feel, or touch-- but Eternity is not just a nebulous state in our minds of a place that is somewhere out there in the future. We can't worry about it when we get around to it.

I want that same fire that burned in those men and women of God that gave them that grasp of the reality of the Gospel. I don't want to get around to it after I've satiated myself with the life that is around me. I want to walk in the Spirit of God now.

What else is there in life that is really worth living for anyway? There is no lasting value in fame, fortune, or pleasure. What excitement can this life offer that will compare with the glory of entering into the presence of God? And yet, it is so easy to get caught up in what we see around us.

We need an old-fashioned, Heaven-sent, on-fire, Holy Ghost Revival. And we need some heroes that have a grasp of the reality of Eternity to stand in the power and authority of God that will proclaim the power of God unto salvation to anyone who is willing to let loose of their grasp of this world and grab onto the next.

It is the last verse in this chapter that really gets me, however.

"..that they without us should not be made perfect."

What a great thing that God has provided for us in the here and now, to take the testimony of these incredible heroes on to the final victory.

In A Word

> *Now the end of the commandment is charity out of a pure heart, and of a good conscience, and of faith unfeigned: 1Timothy 1:5*

What's in a word? There are a lot of scriptures that deal with the importance of words, as opposed to ideas. Words can kill, and they can heal. Our profession of faith is in words; we are judged by our words, and we bring forth the Truth of the Gospel with words. The Bible says that we live by every <u>word</u> that proceeds out of the mouth of God. Words are definitely important.

Just as there is a difference between the meanings of the words Faith and Belief, there is also a difference between Love and Charity. Faith goes far beyond believing in something. It denotes action. The word Love sometimes gives us a warm, fuzzy feeling, but Charity is the giving of ourselves out of Love so that souls can be saved. I believe that those old King James translators knew the difference.

There's an old story about William Booth, the founder of the Salvation Army and one of the greatest soul-winners of all time, who was given a sum of money one December to send a Christmas greeting to every one of his outposts around the world. Unfortunately, there was only enough money to send one single, solitary word to each of them.

How could he capture the Christmas message in one word? What one solitary word would encapsulate the very essence of Christianity? I dare say, most of us would face quite a challenge with this. Some would say

Faith, some would say Jesus, and others would say Love. There are a variety of choices that allude to all the different aspects of the Gospel that we would like to get across. But what one word would really say it all?

Without hesitation, Booth sent a word that not only measured the depth of this man of God, but set the focus for his entire organization. Can we, as Christians in this community of churches, boast of such single-mindedness? The rest of the above passage in Timothy warns us of swerving aside from this and focusing instead on ourselves, our own goals, our own position, and our own personal needs. Not so long ago, our churches spent their time praying for lost souls to come to salvation. But now, our altar calls are filled instead with people asking for prayer for themselves and the problems they are having with their own lives. Quite a shift in our focus.

And what was William Booth's one solitary word?

"Others."

Perspective

> *Every way of a man is right in his own eyes: but the LORD pondereth the hearts. Proverbs 21:2*

Perspective. Everybody's got one of their own. That's why everyone believes that what they believe in is right. Let's face it, if you didn't believe you were right, you wouldn't believe that way...right? Right! So what about everyone else? Oh, if only they could see things the way you see them, then they would understand. (Or is it the other way around?)

In the scientific community, you start with a basic premise and go about to prove it. When the facts, however, show evidence of something contrary, a good scientist will follow that lead in hopes of discovering the truth. There is no deep, profound assault on his ego by changing his premise-- merely an opportunity to switch to the correct path and perhaps discover something worthy of a Nobel Prize.

In matters of the heart and soul, however, we tend to establish what we have decided to believe and then accept the evidence to prove it. Anything that points to something contrary is often times ignored, dismissed, or rationalized to minimize its significance. We hold on to the beliefs that have found root in our hearts and souls, and we will defend them fiercely. In other words, we will believe what we want to believe.

Sometimes, these are things that we have come to a conclusion about, but often they are just Ideals, mores, and beliefs that we inherited from childhood. We don't always know why we believe them – we just do. And even when it is something that we have figured out for ourselves, we are loath to let it go. It would mean admitting we are wrong.

The heart of man is very deep, the Bible says, and is hard to understand. When it pertains to an idea in our minds, we can switch our position easily; but when it involves a belief that pertains to morals, desires of our hearts, and something that has been planted deeply in our souls, we resist every effort to change. In spite of the facts. Sometimes, even in spite of the Word of God. It takes the active, living Spirit of God to deal with our hearts in order to change us. That is why it is so desperately important for men of God to preach only under the anointing and the Spirit of God. "Life and death are in the power of the tongue."

And that is also why a church that is dead to the Spirit is so lethal to a human soul. (Ephesians 5:11)

Lamentations Coming

"How does the city sit solitary that was full of people." Lamentations 1:1

What if you could look out into the future and see the utter destruction of your people, but no one would listen to you no matter how you cried unto them? Consider how Jeremiah felt as he watched Jerusalem destroyed and carried away to Babylon.

There had been a brief revival during Josiah's reign, but it had been superficial at best because the Jews had gone right back into their carnal ways right after Josiah's death. God could see into the shallowness of their hearts and, during that time of revival, had given Jeremiah repeated warnings of coming destruction. Jeremiah had seemed like a crackpot to them at the time, but now he sat in the midst of the destruction of Mount Zion and mourned for the people of God. They just would not listen to the callings for repentance because their hearts had run after messages of peace and prosperity and had trusted in the fact that they were God's chosen people.

The Jews trusted in their walls as a bulwark against the enemy of their souls, but those walls were broken down, and the enemy had entered into the sanctuary because they were not built upon the righteousness of God. They trusted in brick and mortar instead of heartfelt repentance before God. They didn't think they had been doing anything wrong.

I sincerely believe that we shall see another Babylonian captivity for the Mount Zion of today, the church of Jesus Christ. The scenario is just the same as in the day of Jeremiah – the messages we hear, the attitudes we've developed, the things we trust in for our salvation, and the warnings from God. I expect the results will also be the same. That's a pretty harsh stand to take today when everyone trusts so much in their respective religions. Anyone who is out sounding an alarm of repentance in God's holy mountain looks like a crackpot. Yeah, that hasn't changed, either.

This time, however, we will face the great whore of Revelations, the modern-day Babylon. The Bible says that there will be an hour of temptation that will come to try the whole earth, and most people will submit to this ecumenical move toward a one-world religion. Why? Because they have heard that God is Love, and He wants everyone to love each other so we can have religious peace.

For yourselves know perfectly that the day of the Lord so cometh as a thief in the night. For when they shall say, Peace and safety; then sudden destruction cometh upon them, as travail upon a woman with child; and they shall not escape. 1 Thess. 5:2,3

Believe me, it is coming. It's a lot closer than we would like to think. And it is written so that anyone who has ears to hear can hear.

The enemy is just outside the walls, the battle is set, and so few see the danger.

The Bride

> *"In like manner also, that women adorn themselves in modest apparel, with shamefacedness and sobriety; not with broided hair, or gold, or pearls, or costly array; But (which becometh women professing godliness) with good works."*
>
> *1st Timothy 2: 9,10*

I don't think Paul was trying to tell women how to dress. I realize he wasn't married and didn't know what it was like to live with a woman, but still, he just couldn't be that dumb. I don't think that how you wear your hair, makeup, or earrings are issues of eternal significance. I believe that Paul was addressing the Bride of Christ, the church, that same virtuous woman that we find in Proverbs 31.

Throughout the Bible, we see the same reference to wives as the true church and harlots as false churches. The Book of Proverbs dedicates chapters 5 through 9 as warnings against strange women, who appear as a very nice church that you would like to partake in, but in reality, will take your soul to Hell.

God, from the very beginning, has established the marriage relationship between a man and his wife as the foundational analogy of Christ and His Church. Everything about marriage, from the courtship to the kids, is significant. The Marriage contract is, in essence, a holy vow to serve Jesus Christ.

Having a dead church where you can't feel the moving of the Spirit of God is like having a marriage without sex -- a dead shell instead of a real relationship.

Adultery, Polygamy, modesty, and Maternity are all very significant analogies of our marriage to Jesus Christ.

"Notwithstanding she shall be saved in childbearing..."

Does this mean all women are cursed because of Eve and are destined for Hell if they don't have babies? Does that make any sense at all? Or has it occurred to you that a church that does not win souls is like a wife that is barren, an unfruitful branch on the Vine that is dead and about to be broken off and cast into the fire? The very first commandment God gave was on the fifth Day of Creation – be fruitful and multiply – and that embodies the very essence of Christianity, which is Charity.

Do you belong to a very nice church, but no souls are getting saved there? Nice place, but it's only maintaining the status quo? Perhaps there is something missing in the marriage relationship your church has with Christ.

A church that is not on fire, but is only lukewarm, is a Bride who is in love with someone else other than Jesus Christ. He is looking for a Bride who is passionately in love with Him, and, like Rachael in Genesis 30:1, is desperate to bring forth fruit for her husband.

The Marriage Supper of the Lamb is about to be served. The invitations have been sent, the guests are assembling, and the Bride has made herself ready.

"And the Spirit and the bride say, Come. And let him that heareth say, Come. And let him that is athirst come...."

The Waters of Marah

> *And when they came to Marah, they could not drink of the waters of Marah, for they were bitter:"* Exodus 15:23

Imagine coming out of such an incredible victory as the crossing of the Red Sea and then, just three days later, being faced with your first real test. What? So soon? How could the Lord, who had just wrought such a mighty deliverance, bring the Israelites to such a severe test so soon? But that is just what He did.

Against their murmuring and distrust, Moses did the one thing that the people forgot to do – he cried unto the Lord. The Lord showed him a special tree, just like the tree upon which Jesus was crucified, that healed the waters. The Lord immediately gave them the conditions for their continuing deliverance. They had to remain faithful and keep His commandments. If they would, He said He would place none of the diseases upon them that He had placed upon the Egyptians -- trust Him, follow Him, and keep His commandments, and He would deliver them from the curses that result from sin.

Once they had gone through the testing at Marah, it was then that He brought them to an oasis that had twelve fountains of water and seventy palm trees.

The numbers twelve and seventy are significant throughout the Bible, but suffice it to say that this is the oasis that we desire to come to in our Christian life. But first, we must be proved at Marah. Our Christian walk does not end at the shores of the Red Sea – that is just the beginning. As Christians, our life changes dramatically at the point of Salvation, but there are still many times of trial ahead of us where we will have to trust in God. The Promised Land is still ahead of us, and we still have many trials and tribulations to go through before we enter in. We will come to places like Marah in our walk with God, and we will wonder why He is putting us through this, but it is only a time of trial and testing.

The real significance of Marah is that this was the place where God made a deal with His people. No conditions were placed upon the Jews at the Red Sea. They had no choice. They were thrust out of Egypt and led across the sea, but it was at Marah where the Lord first gave them the conditions for their continued walk with Him. It is at Marah where we are really faced with a choice to serve the Lord or not.

There are conditions that are laid upon us, and we have choices to make if we are to make it all the way to the Promised Land. The Cross can heal the bitterness, but it is our decision to continue to follow the Lord and keep His ways that will bring us to the oasis and, ultimately, Heaven.

And He Could There Do No Mighty Work

> *"And he could there do no mighty work, save that he laid his hands upon a few sick folk, and healed them."* (Mark 6:5)

All he could do was heal a few sick folk? Boy, that would have been enough to get me all excited. But the people in that town just didn't get it. And Jesus marveled because of their unbelief. What more did they want? There was an underlying problem with these people that kept them from experiencing a great move of God. What was the matter with these people? But then, haven't we seen the same today?

Do you believe in the supernatural power of God's ability to heal? Do you really believe? What's more, do you care? I've been in situations here where people have been supernaturally healed when we prayed for them, and yet it generated very little excitement in the Christians that knew about it. Why is that?

There was the girl who had been diagnosed with 62 distinct demonic personalities who had come crying for help, and the Lord delivered her with a gigantic "whoosh" when we prayed for her. There was the little girl who had AIDS with little time to live that the Lord healed instantly. Then there was the man who had leukemia so bad that his head was swollen like a basketball. He could take you to the very spot where he was standing when the Lord crashed down on him and completely healed him. And there are many more.

This is pretty supernatural stuff! And it happens today just like it did in Jesus' time. But what's the reaction of Christians and of ministers who hear about things like this? "Oh, that's nice." Ho-hum. That's nice? You know what, I also marvel.

I am convinced that the underlying problem is that, since it didn't happen to them personally, it doesn't have quite the same effect. Human nature makes us generally more concerned with ourselves than with others. It's a fact of life. And it shows itself in the type of Gospel that we hear preached over our pulpits today and the resulting effect it has on our lives.

We flock by the thousands to ministries that preach a "feel good" message and tell us "smooth" things. Prosperity ministries abound and make no pretense about what their focus is on. We love to hear that God loves us and that we can rest in a permissive gospel. And when we gather up at the front of the altar on Sunday, what is it that everyone prays for? Themselves -- their own problems, their own needs, and their own desires. Some altar call that is. Every once in a while, someone will throw out a bone for lost souls, but it's usually something quick so we can get back to praying for ourselves.

Think I'm being cynical? Take a circuit tour of our churches and see if I'm not telling the truth.

Real revival never comes to those who are satisfied and are only concerned with their own well-being. It comes to those who, in desperate prayer and crying out to God from the depths of their hearts for others, want more than "church as usual" and who are willing to pay whatever price to see souls come to Salvation and escape the horrors of Hell for eternity.

There are those of you who are out there and are desperate for a move of God. Don't be discouraged.

DALEN GARRIS

Keep storming the Throne of God. Mighty works are on the way.

Dumb Peter

Did you ever wonder if Peter wished that all the dumb stuff that he had said wasn't written in the Bible for everyone to see? He really did come off with quite a few of them. But then, heck, he was only a dumb fisherman.

Peter may not have been very bright, and he certainly wasn't very educated, but he knew Jesus. He did not have a Ph.D. and was not a real strong candidate for the Sanhedrin, the high order of the religious council. Neither was he very smooth in his approach toward things, but he knew the Truth.

In our approach to God, there is a vast difference in whether it is with our minds or with our hearts. And it is reflected in the difference between the two Trees in the Garden of Eden – the Tree of Life and the Tree of Knowledge. One is with our hearts; one is with our minds. One is spiritual; one is carnal. One is Life; one is Death. Peter chose Life.

When you get to the Judgment Bar of God, there will not be a quiz on how much you know or who you are. Ph.D.'s and other ecclesiastical heavyweights won't count for much. As a matter of fact, Jesus said that God hid these things from the wise and prudent and revealed them unto babes. Good thing, because otherwise, only the smart and the educated would go to Heaven. The rest of us dumb clucks would wind up in Hell.

What is wisdom, then?

Job says, "And unto man he said, Behold, the fear of the Lord, that is wisdom; and to depart from evil is understanding." Isn't it just like God to turn things all around like that?

As for Peter? Poor, dumb, unsophisticated, uneducated, rude, and crude Peter? Well, Jesus said that Peter would sit on one of the twelve thrones, judging the twelve tribes of Israel.

Not bad for a poor, dumb fisherman. Not bad at all.

Stand

> *"If you don't stand for somethin', you'll fall for anything..." (Popular Country song)*

How true. Just to know something is right is not enough. You have to make a stand for what you believe in. Some people only believe in themselves, and the stand they make in life is only for their own success, their career, their security, or their own fun and pleasure. That's what drives their lives.

Others are not sure what to believe in. They hear the old story of the blind men feeling the elephant, each grabbing a different part and thinking that the elephant is what they perceive it to be. In other words, everybody is right, and nobody is wrong. (Sounds a lot like Outcome Based Education.) They are fond of quoting the Hindu *Bhagavad Gita* which says there's a many-twined rope that leads to heaven. Whichever way you choose is okay, I guess. Hey, I've got an idea! Let's have a one-world religion. That way, everybody can be right!

But Jesus said that there was only one way. Eternity is not dependent upon a grocery store mentality. You can't just walk down the aisles and pick whatever suits your preferences. Either it is the Truth, or it's not. If there are 50,000 different truths, then there is no absolute Truth at all, and if so, nothing really matters anyway.

But there is an absolute Truth, and it does matter. Jesus spoke to us from an empty grave. No other "truth" can boast of the power of resurrection. And when He spoke to us through His Word, He meant exactly what He said. There aren't different versions, different perspectives, different flavors, or different preferences. There is a right way and a wrong way, and the consequences of your choice will be felt for Eternity.

When you find the Truth, however, the question remains, will you stand for it, or will you just acknowledge that it is correct?

> "...*earnestly contend for the truth that was once delivered unto the saints.*" Jude 1:3

THE NEW SCHOOL PRAYER

This was written by a teenager in Baghdad, Arizona. Many of you may have already heard this, but many have not. I think the fact that this is coming from the heart of one of our own children makes this especially poignant and worthy of passing on. How far have we fallen that our children would have to make this kind of cry? And how will we answer God?

> *Now I sit me down in school*
> *Where praying is against the rule.*
> *For this great nation under God*
> *Finds mention of Him very odd.*
> *If Scripture now the class recites,*
> *It violates the Bill of Rights.*
> *And anytime my head I bow,*
> *Becomes a Federal matter now.*
> *Our hair can be purple, orange or green.*
> *That's no offense; it's a freedom scene.*
> *The law is specific; the law is precise.*
> *Prayers spoken aloud are a serious vice.*
> *For praying in a public hall*
> *Might offend someone with no faith at all.*
> *In silence alone, we must meditate,*
> *God's name is prohibited by the state.*
> *We're allowed to cuss and dress like freaks,*
> *And pierce our noses, tongues and cheeks.*
> *They'll outlawed guns, but FIRST the Bible.*
> *To quote the Good Book makes me liable.*

DALEN GARRIS

We can elect a pregnant Senior Queen,
And the 'unwed daddy', our Senior King.
It's "inappropriate" to teach right from wrong,
We're taught that such "judgments" do not belong.
We can get our condoms and birth controls,
Study witchcraft, vampires and totem poles.
But the Ten Commandments are not allowed,
No word of God must reach this crowd.
It's scary here, I must confess,
When chaos reigns, the school's a mess.
So, Lord, this silent plea I make:
Should I be shot; My soul please take!

Amen

Convict our hearts, O God. Forgive us, and give us the courage to take a stand for the things we know are right, regardless of the cost, regardless of what we are told is unlawful, regardless of what <u>anyone</u> says, so that our children do not have to grow up in such a world as this that has lost its moral compass.

The Alabaster Box

> "...one thing is needful, and Mary hath chosen that good part."

As Jesus sat in Simon's house, a woman came and broke an alabaster box and anointed him, not only with very precious spikenard, but also with her tears. She knew little of the intricacies of the Gospel, understood little of the incredible Messianic prophesies, had no grasp of the eternal plan of God, and had neither degree nor position in the ecclesiastical church. But she knew that Jesus was her Lord. The alabaster box that she broke before Him symbolized her heart, and she poured out the ointment of her soul, her most precious possession. Here was worship in purity, sincerity, and truth.

Those standing around were of various positions in life. Judas, of course, objected because he was looking to serve a Christ that would be an earthly conqueror, in whose kingdom he would find a position. This demonstration of humble and contrite worship from the heart was not what he was looking for, and he proceeded to betray Jesus to the chief priests.

There were many Pharisees there who recognized that Jesus was the Master, and they loved the opportunity to engage in theological dissertations about the Word of God with Him. The appeal of analytical knowledge thrilled them, but they were not able to reach beyond to this depth of worship. They only had a form of godliness, a religious "head knowledge" of who He was. They were never able to come to the knowledge of the Truth.

The disciples were there also. A little clueless, perhaps, but nevertheless watching in awe as this woman poured out her heart and soul. I'm sure they loved it, as they loved Jesus, but they had not entered into their ministry yet and had not reached that same depth of soul that this simple woman had.

And then there's us. Where would we be standing in this room? Has it occurred to us that there is a deeper place in God than where we've been? Have we nestled ourselves in the shadow of the Almighty, that secret hiding place in God?

There's so much more to God than just church, but our souls have to be hungry enough to reach out for it. We must be willing to break our stony alabaster hearts and, in the spirit of pure worship, pour out our souls to God.

> *"...Wheresoever this gospel shall be preached throughout the whole world, this also that she has done shall be spoken of for a memorial of her." Mark 14:9*

May the same be spoken of us all.

THE EARLY YEARS

A Father's Agonizing Decision

Let me tell you a story about a father's agonizing decision:

After a few of the usual Sunday evening hymns, the church's pastor slowly stood up, walked over to the pulpit, and introduced his childhood friend.

With that, an elderly man stepped up to the pulpit to speak, "A father, his son, and a friend of his son were sailing off the Pacific Coast," he began, "when a fast-approaching storm blocked any attempt to get back to shore. The waves were so high that even though the father was an experienced sailor, he could not keep the boat upright, and the three were swept into the ocean."

The old man hesitated for a moment, making eye contact with two teenagers who were, for the first time since the service began, looking somewhat interested in his story. He continued, "Grabbing a rescue line, the father had to make the most excruciating decision of his life....to which boy he would throw the other end of the line. He only had seconds to make the decision. The father knew that his son was a Christian, and he also knew that his son's friend was not. The agony of his decision could not be matched by the torrent of waves. As the father yelled out, 'I love you, son!' he threw the line to his son's friend. By the time he pulled the friend back to the capsized boat, his son had disappeared beyond the raging swells into the black of night. His body was never recovered."

By this time, the two teenagers were sitting straighter in the pew, waiting for the next words to come out of the old man's mouth. "The father," he continued, "knew his son would step into eternity with Jesus, and he could not bear the thought of his son's friend stepping into an eternity in Hell. Therefore, he sacrificed his son. How great is the love of God that He should do the same for us." With that, the old man turned and sat back down in his chair as silence filled the room.

Within minutes after the service ended, the two teenagers were at the old man's side. "That was a nice story," politely started one of the boys, "but I don't think it was very realistic for a father to give up his son's life in hopes that the other boy would become a Christian."

"Well, you've got a point there," the old man replied, glancing down at his worn Bible. A big smile broadened his narrow face, and he once again looked up at the boys and said, "It sure isn't very realistic, is it? But I'm standing here today to tell you that THAT story gives me a glimpse of what it must have been like for God to give up His Son for me.

You see....I was the son's friend."

Ol' Blind Bartimaeus

> *"And they came to Jericho: and as he went out of Jericho with his disciples and a great number of people, blind Bartimaeus, the son of Timaeus, sat by the highway side begging."* Mark 10:46

Ol' blind Bartimaeus. I wonder how long he had sat there over the years, blind and without hope, begging for pennies to sustain himself. Had anyone ever paid him any notice over those years? A penny here and a penny there, but really, he was just an anomaly of society, an old blind beggar that nobody really gave much thought to, sitting by the side of the road of Life without hope.

There was no welfare for the blind and no medicine that could heal them in those days. Bartimaeus was condemned to a miserable, scant existence as a beggar, left to sit on the side of a dusty road in poverty until he finally died and was carried out of the way.

But then Jesus came by.

The very last thread that your heart hangs onto is hope. You can lose your health, your money, your respect, your family, your happiness, and even your faith, but when you lose hope, there is nothing left. Blind Bartimaeus hung on, in desperation, to a last thread of hope that there could be deliverance in this man Christ Jesus; that somehow, in all of God's mercy, there really could be a way out.

He didn't ask for money, a job, a social position, or even food. He wanted to see! Oh, if only he could just see! Nothing else mattered. It didn't matter that everybody told him to shut up. He was, after all, just a lowly beggar. Why trouble the Master? Mind your place, Bartimaeus! But a hope that he had thought was completely gone had sprung up in his heart, which had been so dark for so long, and nothing would shut him up.

"Jesus, thou son of David, have mercy on me."

And out of all the noise and commotion of all the crowds of people, Jesus heard that one solitary voice crying out for help.

We don't have beggars sitting on the side of the road anymore, but we sure have a lot of people who are blind and cannot see; people that have just about lost hope that there could ever be deliverance from the misery of sin. We may see with our eyes, but our perception of life, reality, and eternity can be clouded with the confusion of this life so that there is no Light in our lives. We may be financially secure, but our souls can be desperately poor for the Truth, and we are left sitting by the highway of Life begging for crumbs.

No matter how hopeless life may seem to you, just remember ol' blind Bartimaeus.

He took hold of a hope that was gone, cried out with all his heart, and Jesus heard him.

The Gospel According to Rene Descartes

Rene Descartes was the philosopher who wrote the famous phrase, "I think, therefore I am," to expose the nature of our existence in this Universe. It's a formidable work and hard for the average guy to follow along. Nevertheless, it has influenced much of modern thought. But to know that God exists does not make you a Christian.

In today's Christian America, we have been exposed to the Gospel from our youth up. We have built churches everywhere and have sent missionaries all over the world. Yet all that this has accomplished is to make us accountable. We have heard. We know. We understand. But does this make us righteous before God?

I have heard repeatedly, especially from people here in the Bible Belt, that because they believe in God, they therefore assume that they are going to Heaven when they die. ("I believe, therefore I'm saved"). Is this really what the Bible preaches? Or is there something more to being a Christian than just being a "hearer of the Word"? (James 1:23)

Human nature seeks equilibrium -- a place of security and peace. We strive to find that place where we can rest from our troubles and labor and finally relax. We would much rather hear a message of peace and prosperity than endure a doctrine that requires us to strive to overcome. It's our nature.

To "relax and be raptured" sounds so good, but the Bible preaches a message of enduring conflict. It starts in Genesis and ends in Revelations. The Bible says, "there is no discharge from that war" (Ecclesiastes 8:8). War it is, and war it will be until it is finally all over. We have an adversary, the Devil, and he will not relax until the end. His primary weapon is flattery and temptation to get us to relax while he works feverishly to deceive us.

But there is a rest to the people of God, and it is on the Cross. As Jesus rested from His work on the Cross, so are we exhorted to also walk that same crucified walk of the lowly Nazarene. If we will rest from our own works and the way we would do things and instead take upon ourselves to walk in His Spirit, then we allow Him to give us the power to work the works of God.

You will not find true rest anywhere else.

The Cycle of Apostasy

And an angel of the LORD came up from Gilgal to Bochim, and said, I made you to go up out of Egypt, and have brought you unto the land which I sware unto your fathers; and I said, I will never break my covenant with you.

And ye shall make no league with the inhabitants of this land; ye shall throw down their altars: but ye have not obeyed my voice: why have ye done this? Judges 2:1,2

The answer is Compromise. Religious compromise is the tendency of human nature to shy away from spiritual warfare. There is a cycle that repeats itself throughout the Word of God. One generation answers the call of God to charge into the battle; the next generation enjoys the fruits of their victory, and then the next set of generations relaxes into apostasy and compromise.

Then God sends prophets to call His people to repentance. They persecute and kill those whom the Lord has sent, but a seed grows out of that persecution, and another generation will rise up to answer the call to battle again. Over and over again, the cycle repeats itself.

Victory does not come through compromise but through warriors that will make a stand for Truth. The call to repentance never seems to come from established institutions, but rather, the Lord calls forth his prophets out of nowhere without any recognized credentials. That is true from Moses, through the prophets, to John the Baptist, Jesus, and through the apostles unto today.

He even used a jackass at one point.

Why is that? Could it be that it is not the messenger that is important, but rather the message? Is it because the Lord is looking for those who will respond to righteousness and Truth instead of some exalted celebrity's personality? Or is it because religious organizations tend to fall into the slack part of that cycle of apostasy?

I believe we are in the slack part of the last one of those cycles. Churches are on every corner, but there is a lack of a manifestation of the power of God and hardly any call to battle. Everywhere I turn, I hear of preachers encouraging their people to "put aside their petty differences" and to have "unity with all the churches, but Ephesians chapter 4 talks of the unity of the Body of Christ through righteousness and walking in the Spirit of God – not through compromise. There is no compromise with the Devil.

While many are looking with apprehension for bombs, tanks, and UN troops, the Word of God tells us that the Antichrist will win the kingdom with flatteries. Many will fall for this unified one-world church movement.

And there is a stirring in the graveyard as our church fathers roll over in their graves.

The Emperor's Clothes

By Jim Hunt

The world is a much more interesting and honest place when viewed through the eyes of young children. With vivid imagination, they can slip into the realm of fantasy for hours and then suddenly, seemingly at will, return to the reality of the present with utterly disarming candor. I have observed this in my own little ones, marveling as they grow through the stages of discovery, wonder, and observation, developing perspective and perception intuitively.

Not bound by the mincing of words and "political correctness" that we adults are slaves to, children have that uncanny knack for seeing and stating things as they really are, rather than the way they ideally <u>should</u> be. Popular literature alludes to this phenomenon in such classics as "The Emperor's New Clothes" which recounts the tale of a gullible emperor who is persuaded by clever knaves that his special new apparel is visible to any intelligent person and *invisible* only to a fool. No one, ruler or subject, will admit to being unable to see this alleged magical outfit, and all pretend to admire it, not wanting to appear foolish, even though they can't really see any such garment at all. Finally, a little child states the obvious: "But the emperor isn't wearing any clothes." Eventually, everyone whispers the truth to one another, and the charade is ended.

It may be a fairy tale, but the author was certainly expressing some accurate insight into the ways of children. They can be brutally, but refreshingly, honest.

One sunny day last summer, this truth was brought

home to me on a personal note. I was having a pleasant afternoon in the backyard with my children when one of the swings came apart under especially rigorous use. After repairing the broken swing, I decided to test it out with my own ample body weight to make sure no small fry would get hurt.

Renee, age seven, giggled, "Grandpa, you'd better stay off that swing. You're just too fat". Noah, my six-year-old rebuked her immediately: "Renee, you shouldn't call old people fat … it hurts their feelings." My self-esteem thus salvaged, and my honor so valiantly defended, I paused a moment to reflect how delightful it would be to be that age again and have the freedom to say what I really thought. Now that's freedom of speech!

Noah also has a massive collection of small plastic animals, primarily dinosaurs, lizards, bugs of every description, and a smattering of the whole animal kingdom, the culmination of many trips to the 99-cent store. They have been assigned names and personalities and are the key players in countless mini-dramas played out on the "jungle mat" in Noah's bedroom.

Once these animals are laid out in some array, disturbing them (for some arcane purpose such as vacuuming the room) would be akin to wiping out an entire civilization. Any allusion to the idea that they are not living beings with feelings and sensitivity is absolute heresy.

One day Noah took his menagerie on an excursion to the basement. Carrying them gingerly in a box, he was on the stairs when the box tumbled to the bottom, spilling everything unceremoniously down the stairwell. Concerned that he would be upset, I rushed to offer my condolences: "Everyone ok there?" "Dad," Noah replied, "don't worry … they're just little pieces of plastic."

Hmm…just when I thought I was getting the hang of it.

Hector, the Soul Collector

A good friend of mine, John, spent his time in Vietnam as a machine-gunner in the Marines. After all the bloodshed of battle, he would go into the Chapel to light candles, burn incense, genuflect, and count his prayer beads. The contradiction really started bothering him, so one day, he asked the Chaplain if there wasn't something wrong here -- say your prayers to God, and then go into the jungle and "light up Charlie."

The answer he got back was that he was fighting for God. He thought that sounded pretty cool, so he named his machine gun "Hector, the Soul Collector." He figured that he was doing the Viet Cong a favor by sending them off to meet God and adopted the attitude of "kill 'em all, and let God sort 'em out."

It has never ceased to amaze me how human nature can believe anything, even the most bizarre ideas, as long as it exonerates you from the conviction of sin and soothes your conscience. People can find a way to believe what they want to believe, in spite of the facts or common sense.

At some point in our lives, however, we will come face to face with that rigid wall of God's Truth. Either we accept it, or we can look for ways around it. Either we can shrug off that Holy Ghost conviction like an uncomfortable garment, or we can humble ourselves in fear of God and allow our wills to be broken through repentance.

When you know that God is really there but don't want to yield to His Word, it is often easier to fall into a religion that will make you feel better about yourself.

That way, you can say you're religious, but you don't really have to walk in fear of the Lord. That's why you will see thousands flock to preachers that have smooth, "feel good" ministries and scorn ministers of righteousness who preach repentance.

It was the same trick in the Garden of Eden. *"Thou shalt not surely die."* It worked then, and it still works today.

As for John, he met the Lord Jesus Christ as his personal Savior and traded Hector in for the Word of God. He's still a Soul Collector, but now he's out there on the streets of L.A. getting them <u>before</u> they die.

"Every way of a man is right in his own eyes: but the Lord pondereth the hearts." Proverbs 21.2

Prophets

> *And it shall come to pass in that day, that the prophets shall be ashamed every one of his vision, when he hath prophesied; neither shall they wear a rough garment to deceive: Zechariah 13:4*

It seems that we are always hearing about some new "Prophetic Ministry" that has risen up. Our first natural reaction is to be excited to hear some new word from God. So many times, however, we only hear the same message that we've already heard from the last "prophetic ministry." The themes usually center on wonderful promises of all the good things that God is going to do for us shortly, and we leave feeling really good about ourselves. Often, these people with this "gift of prophecy" will tell us something personal in our lives that is coming. We're getting a new car, or we will soon take a trip, or there will be a change in our lives. How wonderful to get to hear a personal message straight to us from God Himself. It's almost like having your own personal Christian horoscope.

Rarely do we hear prophetic messages of "doom and gloom," judgment, repentance, and the Fear of the Lord. Those kinds of messages don't draw crowds, and they sure don't sell tickets. We don't want to hear bad stuff; we want to hear the good stuff. We don't want to hear something that will make us afraid; we want to hear something that makes us feel good. As we see crowds flocking to these "feel good" ministries, we see more and more of these "prophetic" ministries pop up.

Is that really what prophets of God are supposed to be like? Are prophets now become little more than fortunetellers and entertainers? How do they and their messages measure up against the prophets in the Bible and the kinds of messages that they brought forth?

I have an old saying, "Everybody wants to be an Elijah, but nobody wants to pay the price." I don't see any of the prophets in the Bible jumping up and down for joy over the calling that was placed upon them. The job of a prophet is hard, and the price that is required is more than what human flesh wants to pay.

Ezekiel tells us that the real job of a prophet is to stand in the gaps of the walls that are broken down and call the people of God back to repentance. Micah says that it is to declare unto them their sin and transgression. Foretelling what is to come is not the job of a prophet; it is the consequence of the job. They don't give messages to make you feel comfortable; they give you messages to make you feel uncomfortable. It is a small wonder, then, that real prophets are always despised.

Only in times of severe persecution and affliction, does God send messages of peace and conciliation to encourage and strengthen His people to hold on to His promises. In times of prosperity and relative peace, however, the message is about repentance and coming judgments.

Most of what we hear today, however, are messages of prosperity, peace, love, and beautiful things. There are severe sentences of judgment written in the Bible for false prophets that prophesy Peace when the Lord had not spoken through them.

A wise man loves reproof, Proverbs says. I'd rather have God drag me off to the ol' woodshed any day and scare the Devil out of me than be appeased by Gypsy fortune-tellers that weaken my resolve to seek the face of God in fear and trembling.

The Making of a Prophet

Jeremiah was called right in the midst of the great revival during Josiah's reign. Everything was looking so good ... on the surface. Everybody that was anybody was going to church, they had just had the greatest Passover since the days of Joshua, and nobody was expecting messages of "doom and gloom." All the so-called prophets of the time were foretelling of peace, prosperity, and good things. Life was good. They were filled with prosperity, and danger seemed a long way off.

"You want me to tell them *WHAT*?"

No matter how much Jeremiah squirmed, God was not taking excuses. The severe prophesies and judgments that God gave to Jeremiah to deliver may not have made sense to the carnal mind, but God had a different perspective and could see past the surface into people's hearts. He told Jeremiah that either he told these people what he was told to tell them, or God was going to break Jeremiah down in front of everybody. He was going to do it or else.

You know what? Jeremiah did it. And he did it for the next 30 or so years, all the while knowing how few would believe him. He was mocked, persecuted, ignored, and thrown down into the bottom of a well. But he told them. He didn't do it because he understood the grand scheme of things or how everything fit together. He did it because he knew it was the truth.

He did it because he feared God more than he feared public opinion.

Famine

> *"Woe to them that are at ease in Zion... but they are not grieved for the affliction of Joseph."* Amos 6:1,6

We are living in the days that have been prophesied just before that great and terrible day of the Lord comes. While we may see singing and dancing in our churches, yet the prophecies in the Word of God keep rolling on like a great stone wheel of judgment.

These are times of famine. We have all heard of some of the great moves of God in the past and enjoy the retelling of stories of tremendous deliverance, of outpourings of the Holy Ghost where the Spirit was as thick as fog, and of multitudes of souls coming down to the altars in deep, broken repentance. What wonderful stories. And there are old-timers amongst us that remember because they were there. But they're just stories to us.

The Book of Joel says that the Lord would cut off the corn, the wine, and the oil from the houses of joy, and Amos says that we would experience a famine for hearing the Word of God. Spiritual desolation has crept in upon us; we have a dry desert instead of the lush, blossoming fields of revival. This is that which Paul spoke of when he said that, in the last days, Christians would no longer endure sound doctrine but would heap up to themselves teachers that would preach unto them the smooth messages of love, peace, and prosperity that their ears itch to hear. And they would turn their ears away from hearing the Truth.

Thus, the famine. He said He would rain upon one

city and not the other, just to make it evident that the Spirit of God is still real, but they still would not return to that deep walk in the righteousness of God.

These are those "perilous times" of the last days that the Bible warns us of. Religion becomes the most dangerous thing on earth when it leads to "church as usual" -- a nice, easy-going gospel without the fear of God, without an understanding of Hell, and the resulting leanness of soul.

Only through repentance does a real move of God ever come. But our altar calls today have only become a gathering together at the end of a wishy-washy message to hug each other and complain about all our problems. With as many churches as we have, how many altar calls do we see for the lost? How many calls to repentance do we ever hear? And how many souls are cut to the heart with Holy Ghost conviction for an outpouring of the latter rain?

Does that offend you? Good. Let it goad you to storm the Throne of God like Nehemiah did to cry for a restoration of the Church. Let us rise up in the Spirit of the Lord and storm the Throne of God for repentance and for one last great revival before it is all too late.

Therefore also now, saith the LORD, turn ye even to me with all your heart, and with fasting, and with weeping, and with mourning: And rend your heart, and not your garments, and turn unto the LORD your God: for he is gracious and merciful, slow to anger, and of great kindness, and repenteth him of the evil. (Joel 2:12-13)

Mahershalalhasbaz

> "...and she conceived, and bare a son. Then said the Lord to me, Call his name Mahershalalhashbaz." (Isaiah 8:3)

And for a nickname? One thing's for sure. There won't be any other kids in his class with the same name. You won't find this one in those little books about what to name your baby.

I sometimes wonder what ever happened to Maher...whats-his-name. His father, Isaiah, had a pretty tough job, and they lived at some very tumultuous times. It has been said that they finally killed Isaiah by boiling him in oil. How did that affect Mahershalalhashbaz? With a name like that, he surely stood out in the crowd, but did he stand up against the crowd? Did he inherit the strength and faith of his father?

How about Job's kids? The Bible says that, at the end, he had seven sons and three daughters. (There go the keys to the car!) Did they understand what Job had gone through to establish the sovereign authority of God? After all, they were only there during the times of Job's blessings. They never got to see the times of adversity.

Isaac and Rebecca had their problems with kids, too. Esau had taken a couple of wives that the Bible says were a grief unto them. Was this just another case of problems with the in-laws? Or was it that their first-born son just didn't inherit the same vision and faith that was in his parents?

Written into the laws of God are repeated admonitions to deliver unto our children the great truths of the Word of God, His great and mighty acts and deliverances, and to make them understand the righteousness and the judgments of God. There's a reason for that. We were there; they weren't. We got to see it first-hand; they have only heard the tales. Somehow, we have to transfer the vision, the faith, and the excitement to our children, because if we don't, who will?

How much like the successive ages of the churches, even all the way back to the times of Joshua. Just 70 to 80 years ago, we had wave after wave of excitement pass through our country. Religious fervor was at an all-time high; Revivals were on fire everywhere. Souls were coming to the Lord by the thousands, multitudes of sick were supernaturally healed, and the Lord was breathing life into the soul of our nation.

Does anyone remember? Or have we just heard the stories and are content to sit in our status quo and wait? Does the blame fall on our fathers for not instilling the fear of the Lord in us? Or, like wayward children who would not listen, have we been more enamored with the glitter of this world, the success of life, and the instant gratification of the flesh?

A generation that has not fed off the fire of God will look everywhere else for rest but will never find it. Eventually, after enough lost generations have wandered far enough and long enough, they will come back to the original fountain of life that can be found, not in Religion, but only in the breath of the Spirit of God.

I am looking forward to a great revival in this last

generation. They have been starved long enough with a diet of traditional church and a weak gospel without any real power. They are hungry for the fire that comes from off the altar of God.

Once it begins to flow, there will be an army of Christian warriors that will rise up like has never been seen, and we will have the greatest revival of all time.

Hatred

> *He that hateth dissembleth with his lips, and layeth up deceit within him; When he speaketh fair, believe him not: for there are seven abominations in his heart.*
>
> *(Proverbs 26:24,25)*

Recently, I spent an afternoon with a friend who had for years held onto a deep root of bitterness against someone. He had suffered a lot because of this other person and looked upon many years of his life as being ruined spiritually, emotionally, and financially. It had affected every part of his life and the lives of his family. The bitterness had grown into hatred and was festering deep inside him.

Although he could admit how much he hated this other person, he would not admit to being bitter. I was a bit stunned at how he could separate the two. I began to realize that the hatred had become justified in his mind and had taken on a holy character. It had now assumed the robes of righteous indignation. The murderer had become the crusader.

It is true that the fear of the Lord is to hate evil, and that the Bible says that Lord really does hate the workers of iniquity. There is a difference, however, between righteous indignation that is born out of a holiness that despises sin, and a personal wound that festers with the poison of pride and revenge. One makes you strong; the other destroys your soul.

Bitterness has a way of eating a person from the inside and destroying them in such a way that they cannot see it themselves. That is the great deceit of hatred – it secretly destroys the one that hates without them knowing it. Even when he speaks "fair," there are still seven abominations buried deep in his heart, and he can't be trusted. He is captive to his own destruction.

The Lord cannot use anyone who is captive to hatred and bitterness. Before a person can attain the victory that comes from righteousness, he must destroy those beasts. Hatred is actually a form of lust. Only once you are free from that sin can you ever be used by God to fulfill the calling placed upon your life.

Make no mistake. Judgment awaits us all. And there is none righteous, no not one. But there are those who, realizing their sin, have come to the Cross with a repentant heart and received salvation through the Blood of Jesus Christ to wash away their sins. To be born-again, however, does not give anyone a free ticket into Heaven. What it does give you is the power to overcome sin in any shape or form it comes to you. The power to walk in the newness of the Spirit of God so that you don't have to sin anymore is what Grace is all about. There is no excuse for sin in your life.

The only way to claim victory over hate and bitterness is through deep, broken repentance before the Throne of God. Only through the Blood of Jesus Christ is there victory over sin.

The power to overcome sin and hatred is there. But the choice is yours.

A Touch From the Finger of God.

From Cindy

Our life on earth is mostly a day-by-day existence. Go to the job, get the paycheck, pay the bills, cook the meals, juggle the schedules, and so on! It isn't as dreary as it sounds on paper because in between the routines are the little bumps of emergencies, the big crisis, or the surge of excitement and joy. We gain depth, strength, and insight from the valley trials; we gain encouragement and joy in the Lord from the mountaintop victories. In the middle are the "light-as-a-feather" touches from the finger of God.

That is what happened this weekend at our house: a touch of God's finger upon us. Everyone from our part of Texas had gathered at our house for a quick visit from out-of-town friends. This quickie visit had been planned for three weeks, and there was an air of anticipation that was more than the usual excitement. The hope for good food and good fellowship far exceeded our plans. Every person went home with a revitalized spirit, refreshed in the Lord, filled with good memories, and armed with new insight and weapons against Satan.

We talked about old times (good and bad), all our children and grandchildren, our current happenings, and our goals and hopes. When we prayed for each other in specific areas, there was an urgency and flowing of the Spirit that just got everyone's zeal going.

So, what happened this time that made this a glowing weekend? The way I feel today is that God looked down on our tiny spot on earth and gave us a glittering dewdrop from heaven that just enveloped everything and everybody. So even though our life on earth is a day-by-day routine, we also have a daily walk with God. And sometimes, in the middle of an average day, we are rewarded with special treats like a touch from the finger of God.

> *Then he said unto them, Go your way, eat the fat, and drink the sweet, and send portions unto them for whom nothing is prepared: for this day is holy unto our Lord: neither be ye sorry; for the joy of the Lord is your strength. Nehemiah 8:10*

Worship

Worship. Real, pure, deep abject worship. It is the thing that made the difference between Saul and David; it is the quality that turns a believer into a servant, and it is the flame that burns on the altar of our hearts. It's the pure essence of our Faith.

While the disciples stood around clueless in Simon the leper's house, Mary found a place of immortality with Him when she broke the alabaster box of her heart, anointed Him with that precious ointment, and washed His feet with her tears. It touched God's heart. In the midst of the ecclesiastical theologians and faithful disciples, her act of worship gave off the one sweet fragrance of praise that He really savored. There is an element to praise and worship that can never be duplicated by just singing songs in church. It is borne of an understanding of just who God really is.

Here in the democracies of the 21st Century, we have no grasp of the supreme authority that absolute monarchs had in Biblical times. Being raised in this era of human independence has made it difficult to understand what it was really like for the three Hebrew children in the Book of Daniel to stand before the great King Nebuchadnezzar and defy him to his face. We relate kings to Presidents or other political dictators, but the reality of the awesome power they wielded over men has somehow been lost in the translation of time. We have also lost some of our understanding of the abject fear of God because of this, and, as a result, much of the depth of an understanding of true worship.

If you were to relate to some of the old Prophets, or

even the Apostle Paul, that we now look at God as "our Daddy," they would probably faint from disbelief. The old Prophets of God wrote of Him with trembling hands and warned us to make God our dread. They actually trembled at His Word. These days, we play with translations of the Bible as if it doesn't really matter exactly how you say it as long as it pretty much says the same thing.

One of the more popular witticisms that I have heard from many Pastors today is their description of the fear of God as "awesome respect." I wonder how Moses would respond to something like that. He said he feared God so much that his knees smote together! Or how about the Psalmist David, the apple of God's eye? This man, who was so beloved of God, said that the skin on his bones trembled from the fear of God! Maybe that's why he was so beloved.

For those who think that only applies to the Old Testament and to a God that has somehow changed over time, the great Apostle Paul cautions us to serve Him with fear and trembling. He said that "knowing the terror of the Lord, we therefore persuade men."

But today, God is our buddy. He is no longer the awesome holy Monarch who inhabits Eternity and demands the fear of every living soul. Times have changed, and so has the message. God has gotten hip. He's a nice God now. He doesn't hate anymore, has recanted on His Old Testament judgments, and no longer requires holiness in our lives. We know this is true because our preachers have told us so. "God is Love," they say as they proceed into their "feel good" ministries, "and we have nothing to fear because perfect love casts out all fear." So much for Paul's persuasion.

Since God is Love now, we are told that when we do something wrong, it's OK. He understands and winks at us when we "fudge" a little bit. We just have to say we're sorry occasionally, and like a good Daddy, he just puts a Band-Aid on our boo-boo and forgives us. That, from what I'm told by so many loving Christians, is why we love Him so much. How nice. I must remember that.

When we attempt to create God in our own image, however, we lose an essential element of worship. To understand the incredible depth of what Jesus actually did when He humbled Himself to come down and walk among men, you have to know who He really is. You have to understand the vast difference between Spirit and flesh, between holy and profane, between Creator and creation, and between God and man. When we start to catch a mere glimpse of this, we begin to understand the fear of God. When we do not, fear becomes respect, faith is a mere presumption, "God" becomes "our Daddy," Calvary becomes a distant historical event, and worship loses its heart.

Carnalizing God to meet our desired image of Him so we can have a Gospel that does not demand holiness, sacrifice, and fear will not gain us the Love of God our hearts are really seeking for. The Love of God can only be obtained through the fear of God.

The awesome fear of God breeds true worship. Familiarity breeds contempt.

Hem of His Garment

> *"And a certain woman, which had an issue of blood twelve years…"* (Mark 5:25)

Haven't we all had an "issue" of blood? We come into this life and are presented with a whole array of paths that lead to unsure destinations. The goals we sometimes pick, however, have little to do with the real test of Life that we face.

Sin has separated us all from God, and only Salvation can bring us back. It's an issue of blood that is far deeper than our superficial ills. And yet, we continually seek to many physicians to cure us of that nagging ache in our souls. All to no avail. Many of us go through our entire lives without ever understanding what life is really all about.

> *"Rich man, poor man, beggar man, thief; Doctor, lawyer, Indian chief."*

That's great for counting buttons, but in the final analysis, they will not cure the issue of blood that affects our souls. Life on this Earth is not the ultimate goal and purpose. Finding Salvation is.

We are on a journey in life, and this is the time of the year when we stand in the threshold of a doorway into the New Year. We look back wistfully at the year that we have come through, turn, and cinch up our burdens to head down the path that leads down the dim corridor into the next. Will we find what our souls are looking for? Or will we be beset with the many distractions of avenues that lead to physicians that cannot heal and goals that cannot fulfill?

Although we may find temporal comfort in our different stations in Life, it is only when we touch the hem of His garment that we become healed of that issue of blood that plagues our souls.

That woman drove through that crowd of distractions because she knew that only in Jesus Christ would she find what she could never find anywhere else. She touched the hem of His garment, and it gave her life.

The times that are before us are always full of questions and uncertainties, but regardless of where our journey leads us, let us keep our eyes focused on the real issues of life that are before us.

Our journey through this life here is only a test to bring us to our long home in Eternity. It's all a matter of focus -- this world or the next.

The answer and cure lie in the hem of His garment.

Leaves of Grass

Ever watch the wind waving through the fields of grass?

How is it that God is mindful of every blade of grass blowing in the wind? There are fields of grass all over this world, forests that cover continents, and rivers that run for miles, and yet He knows every blade of grass, every drop of water, every sparrow that falls, and every hair on our heads. And He knows every one of our thoughts and the intents of our hearts. Just how great is He, anyway?

One of these days, we will understand. We will all look upon the greatness of God someday, and we will all see Him as He really is. Many of our preconceived notions of what He is supposed to be like will be dissolved at that time, and all the petty things that we concerned ourselves with will seem so stupid. I doubt if there will be one of us that won't lament the time we wasted on things that didn't matter. Our lives will be run, all our causes will have been fought, our time spent, and looming before us will be the great Almighty God in all His glory.

There are times in this life, however, when we wonder where He is. When our lives run through dark, lonely valleys, we sometimes feel like we are all alone and God has abandoned us. Sometimes we have slipped through the dark alleys of sin, not realizing that He was there watching us. And sometimes, we get so enamored with the things of this life that we forget that He is there at all. But He is there.

But sometimes, we just wonder. There are times when it seems hard to remember when we could actually feel the warm Spirit of God falling on us in our worship, when we were reading and discovered miraculous things in His Word, and when our faith was bolstered by the fullness of His presence. There are times when He seems a million miles away, and we wonder.

But He is there. You need to look no further than that blade of grass blowing in the wind.

The Toy Store

Ever watch a mother dragging her 5-year-old through a toy store? Sometimes that's what I feel like in my Christian walk.

Our souls have an inert longing to reach God. Down inside, we really want to serve the Lord and walk deeply in His Spirit, but there is that struggle with our flesh to contend with. There are so many toys out there!

You want to pray – I mean really spend some time reaching the Throne of God and lingering there. You know that is the really important thing in Life, and yet there are all these other things pulling you back into this world. You have to go somewhere; you have to answer the phone; you have to do this; you have to do that. It's like that 5-year-old tugging at your sleeve, trying to get your attention. The checkout counter is right ahead of you, but it's a struggle to get there. If you don't get there, you'll never get out of the store.

Overcoming that tug-of-war is the secret to having an effective Christian walk. That's probably why Jesus said to go into a prayer closet to be alone with God. Slam the door on that 5-year-old kid! It sounds so easy, but let's face it, it is a struggle that we all have to go through.

Did you ever think that maybe the Lord is watching you struggle to see if you will really overcome and choose Him over the things of this world? Talk is cheap, as they say, and actions speak louder than words. According to the Bible, it's not to them that try; it's to them that overcome who will eat of the Tree of Life. The rewards are great, but they aren't cheap and easy.

Last week, a Christian called me to ask if I would go

on a fast with him. It seems he was wrestling with a desire to reach a place in God that he's been trying to get to for quite some time. It sounded more like Holy Ghost conviction than anything else, so I asked him about his prayer life.

"Oh, I pray all day long! My heart is continually crying out to God all day."

"Yeah, but how much time are you spending in serious prayer every day? "

"Well, uh, not really a lot." (Yeah, but he means well, right?)

Praying while you go about your business is like trying to have a deep conversation with someone while you are reading a comic book. Excuse me, but God would like to get your undivided attention for a moment, please. Prayer may be important while you go through your day, but if you don't take some time out to get serious with God, how do you expect Him to get serious with you?

So, I said no. I wasn't going to fast with him to ask God to do the things that God was asking <u>him</u> to do. He had to do it. He could fast his guts out for 50 years, but if he didn't do what the Lord was trying to get him to do, it would be all in vain.

If you ever want to be the effective Christian that your heart cries out to be, you will have to find a way to reach the Throne of God and stay there.

Realizing that we have a continual struggle with the things of this world tugging on us is the first step in overcoming the world. Take steps to make sure you will win that battle. Get up and pray. Get serious with God.

Discipline yourself to take that prayer hour every day no matter what, or you will never attain to that place in God that you long for. There's no way around it.

You have to get past the toys to make it to the checkout counter so you can go home.

New Things

> *"For false Christs and false prophets shall rise, and shew signs and wonders, to seduce, if it were possible, even the elect. But take ye heed: behold, I have foretold you all things."* Mark 13:22,23

It seems that a day doesn't go by where there isn't some new avatar from God with a message about some new thing that has been revealed to him. In every case, the expectation is that we should all drop what we are doing and submit ourselves to this new doctrine, with this new avatar as our new leader, of course.

Some are big avatars; some are little avatars. Some have great and blinding revelations from God; some just "know" the way. It's always some new thing, and they are always supposed to be the anointed leader beguiling unstable souls.

Funny. I don't seem to remember them being around when I got saved. They weren't there when the Spirit of the Lord brought me to life. Where were they when the dynamic outpouring of the Holy Ghost was upon us? As a matter of fact, I have never noticed any evidence of the Spirit of God around them while they are spouting off their new theories.

You know what? I think I'll just stick with what works. Even if an angel of light comes along with a new doctrine, theory, or new way, the Bible says to let him be accursed.

Does that mean that I am not open to new revelations of the Word? Or that I am not willing to correct my own mistakes? Or that I am old-fashioned because I trust in the old paths? Or that I am puffed up because I'm not willing to bend unless I hear from the Lord? No. But I am not going to run after every Pied Piper that calls out to me with some new thing they discovered.

What happens when the satanic spirit of these last days starts giving these weasels the power to conjure up lying signs and wonders? How many unstable souls are going to be swayed by them then? According to the Bible, multitudes will flock to these false prophets. Will you be one of them?

The secret to not being deceived lies, not with good intentions or wishful thinking, but with a determined heart to seek the face of the Lord and to understand His Word. If you don't know what it says, how will you know which is right and which is wrong? Remember, you won't be able to tell by the miracles because they'll be coming from both sides.

In order to fully understand God's Word, you have to be in the Spirit. Simple. It was written in the Spirit; it has to be read in the Spirit. Anything else is just a carnal attempt to read a textbook about God – printed pages with no power. The fullness and depth of the Word of God will only unfold and reveal itself when you yourself are in that same Spirit.

OK, you say. So how do you get in the Spirit so you can immerse yourself in this wonderful spiritual depth? Pray. Is it that simple? Just pray? Well ... sorta.

I guess the real question here is, how much do you want of God? That's how much you need to pray. You get what you pay for. Faith empowers prayer, but prayer opens His Word, which in turn gives you faith, which in turn … you get the idea.

My real point here, however, is that we have entered into an age of deception that will take a lot more spiritual discernment to get through than ever before. If we ignore Jesus' warnings, we will fall prey to these "new" doctrines and false prophets, thinking that we are really more right with God than all those old-fashioned Gospel warriors. And there's only one way to guard against their subtleties: read and pray as if your life depends on it.

Cause it does.

Broken Hearts

Everybody needs something from God – some more desperately than others. The question that begs to be asked is, how do we get God to answer our prayers?

There are those who believe that you can just "name it and claim it." Poof! Bingo-Bango! It's a done deal. You find them running around, laying hands on everybody, claiming all sorts of things in the name of Jesus, and declaring decrees based on their presumptions. But the kingdom of God is not in word but in power. Belief does not constitute Faith. There's more to it than that.

Others believe in a doctrine of works. But that can get really tiring after a while. You can count beads, light candles, say what amounts to "magic words," do good works, and walk little old ladies across the street, but does that ever win you some clout with God to get answers? You might end up feeling good about yourself, but how does that add up when you are desperate for a move from God?

We know that the Book of James tells us that "the effectual fervent prayer of a righteous man availeth much." He speaks of Elijah as a prime example of a man who could get answers from God, but isn't Elijah the same guy who laughed all day long at the Priests of Baal who were jumping around, screaming and yelling for answers from a deaf god? No, there's got to be something more to it than making an outward show of religion.

There is a crucified, broken walk in God that speaks loudly to Him of a heart that is more yielded to His eternal will than anything else. He searches hearts, not heads. There is a depth of poignancy in our hearts that He looks for that goes past everything that is seen on the outside. He looks past our desires to see needs that are colored with a willingness to yield to the will of God in our lives. He looks for hearts that are broken for Him.

Some may say that the Sabbath has to do with the observance of a day of the week. I say that the Sabbath is a place of rest from our own works that can only be attained through a crucified walk in the depth of the Spirit of God. There is a high price to pay to get to that place: total subjection, unquestioned yielding, and complete trust in God.

Creation was not a finished work after seven days -- it was finished on the Cross. As Jesus rested on the Cross, so also does God labor to bring us to that same place in Him – a broken, yielded spirit that is completely given over to the will of God.

Then when we call, He will answer.

"He that dwelleth in the secret place of the most High shall abide under the shadow of the Almighty." Psalms 91

Preparation in Prayer

Prayer is the great hidden generator of a powerful Christian life. As a result, accomplishing an overcoming prayer life is one of the hardest parts of our walk with God. As a friend of mine once answered when asked why it was so hard, "That's easy. Because it's so important!"

You should realize by that statement that I am not talking about simple devotional prayers, saying grace over your food, or "now I lay me down to sleep" prayers. If you ever want to be something in God, you will have to learn how to pray like a warrior. There are no victories without a battle, and there's no battle without conflict, and there will be no conflict if Satan doesn't see your prayer life as a threat.

But so many look upon prayer as a way to get something from God. When do we pray? When we have a need. Gimme, gimme, gimme. If we only look at prayer as a 911 emergency call when we are in trouble, then we will never get to that place of holy communion with Him – that secret place of the Most High God.

If you want to be able to enter the Throne Room of God and know beyond any shadow of doubt that He will stop what He is doing and hold out to you the golden scepter, then you have to have already established an overcoming prayer life – not for you and your needs, but for the Kingdom of God.

I get prayer requests all the time from people who send them out to as many people as they can. Why? Do you think that it's a matter of numbers? Or by chance, hitting upon the right person who has enough faith? Is it a matter of magic words or a certain amount of repetition? Listen folks, either God can hear you or He can't. There's no mysterious formula.

A heart has to be ready to receive anything from God. You may not be ready to be healed, or receive your ministry, or get finances. A loved one may not be ready to get saved just yet. People's hearts have to be prepared to receive anything from God, whether it is wisdom, salvation, miracles, or an answer they are praying for.

In the late '60s and early '70s, multitudes of people flocked to the altars to get saved. Why? Because they were ready for it. The '90s, in contrast, were desolate. Why? Because most people were generally not ready to receive God's kind of Truth. They wanted their own version.

How does this work into the job of a real prayer warrior? There have to be those that are called of God to labor in the intense spiritual warfare of overcoming prayer to prepare the ground. Desperate prayer from strong prayer warriors has to be waged before any battle is to be fought. The priests have to go out before the army of Israel to blow those trumpets.

Faith cannot be turned on like a light switch. Neither can hearts be made ready to receive anything from God by simple wishful thinking. How does one get there? Simple, but not easy. Read and pray. Seek the face of God with all your heart and soul. And get ready to yield to the broken, crucified place in Him that He will bring you to where it will no longer be your will, but the Will of God that rules in your life.

It is a place where you will abide in the suffering of the Body of Christ. The need you then feel will no longer be driven by your own needs but by the very heart of God.

Two Simple Things

"I count all things but loss for the excellency of the knowledge of Christ Jesus my Lord" Philippians 3:8

As carnal creatures, we tend to place more emphasis on carnal things. As a spiritual being, God places more emphasis on spiritual things. The trick is not to get God to conform to us but for us to conform to Him.

We often run around in circles attempting to do all sorts of good deeds, accomplish great church goals, and even make efforts to be a witness to the unsaved. We may feel like we are really serving the Lord when we are able to perceive ourselves as doing something for God, but often what the Lord really wants out of our lives is something much simpler.

Over the years, I've met a lot of zealous men and women who had made Herculean efforts to achieve something in God. When all was said and done, and the excitement had settled, there would be a lot of good deeds, but very often, the anointing of the Holy Ghost was absent. After a time, a lot of hard work would fade into ineffectiveness.

Years of study will produce theologians. Hard work can build a church. Giving money can pay for outreaches of all sorts. But only spiritual warfare, fought and battled down in the trenches of desperate prevailing prayer, can bring forth an outpouring of the Holy Ghost. The real warriors of God find their place of battle down on their knees.

Unless you are in the Spirit, you can accomplish nothing for God. You can preach the Truth, but if you are not standing in the power of God, you will not scare the fleas off a dog. You can resist temptation with all your willpower, but only the power of God can overcome sin. You can't do anything without Him. That's why He will get all the glory.

What you can do, however, are the two simple things that He asks of you:

They are so simple that they are often overlooked. They are so easy that it escapes many people that these two things will really accomplish more than all the good deeds they can muster up. Because it is so little to ask of us, there will be no room for excuses at the Judgment Bar of God for why we didn't do them.

You see, if we would just do these two simple things, everything else would fall into place, and the anointed power of God would then take over. It would then be God that accomplished the work, and not our carnal selves.

Two simple things make all the difference between the carnal and the spiritual – read and pray.

Gideon's Stand

> *And when the men of the city arose early in the morning, behold, the altar of Baal was cast down, and the grove was cut down that was by it, and the second bullock was offered upon the altar that was built.*
> *Judges 6:28*

When God called Gideon, he had been threshing wheat by the winepress. The enemy had infiltrated Israel and had settled in with their farmers, cattle, and homes. They just made themselves at home and, by doing so, had destroyed the increase of God's people.

But Gideon was threshing wheat beside the winepress of God far away from the rest of the people. Sowing unto the Spirit of God in times like these can sometimes only be done in that secret place in God. The world will eat up the spiritual increase by infiltrating the spiritual land of the church, so those whose hearts are devoted to God must thresh beside that secret winepress where the Spirit of the Lord is found.

God had told Gideon to take his father's bullock and sacrifice it and then to break down the altars to Baal. That's like asking you to take your Dad's car and run it off the cliff and then burn down the town's church. If your old man doesn't string you up, the rest of the town will. So, Gideon took ten guys and did it in secret.

Some secret. It lasted until the next day when the angry townspeople squeezed somebody into ratting on Gideon, and they went clamoring for Gideon's blood. They were more afraid of the Amalekites than they were of God Almighty.

The big surprise came when Gideon's Dad made a stand for his son, and in doing so, he also made a stand for his God and his people. Now, he might have whispered into Gideon's ear that, next time, maybe he should ask first before he went sacrificing his father's good cows, but before these so-called "good people" of the land, Gideon's Dad stood his ground.

What are we afraid of when we know that a strong stand for the Truth may not be popular with the crowd? What if we see that the church is willing to allow the world to creep in and settle in their land? What stand will we make?

When we see that the increase has been destroyed and that the miracles and outpouring of the Holy Ghost are no longer evident in our land, we sometimes have to seek unto secret places to thresh our wheat until God calls us forth. But there comes that time when God calls us to make a stand regardless of the consequences.

In times like that, we may be surprised who will be emboldened to stand up alongside us. Gideon may have broken down the altars to Baal, but it was his father who stood up in holy boldness to defend him.

Our Christianity has suffered terribly over the last generation. The churches that had once been forged in the fires of revival are now languishing in complacency – and making excuses for it. Where people used to linger all night in prayer meetings to soak up the anointing, they now gather together to be entertained by motivational speakers. The altar calls that once drew broken-hearted sinners to repentance are now replaced with pity lines for prayer and hugging.

There are distant echoes of thunder from men of

God in the past that preached the strong message of Holy Ghost conviction for sin, but they are drowned out by love messages from "feel good" ministries.

The Amalekites have come in and made themselves at home in our land.

Only those who are willing to risk all for the truth will make a stand in times like these. I believe a Gideon church will rise up in these last days like unto the army written about in the Book of Joel. The battle will be enjoined, and we will have to make a decision on which side we will stand.

Compromise never wins battles.

Once Upon A Time...

Do you know what the difference is between Fairy Tales and Heaven? The Fairy Tales happened once upon a time. Heaven is yet to come ... at least for some of us.

In Fairy Tales, all your dreams come true. You might have to kiss a frog or take care of evil stepsisters while you play with little mice, but somewhere, sometime, somehow, your Prince will always come. Heaven is not quite the same thing. While we all would love the idea of living in a fairy tale existence where everything will be wonderful, reality paints a different picture -- not everything works out according to Walt Disney's script. Life can be tough, and you don't always get to live in a castle, but there is a promise that there really is a place called Heaven. There's only one problem: not everybody is going there. The Prince is coming all right, but He's not taking everybody with Him.

In Fairy Tales, the most wonderful magical things happen for free. Make a wish, and Poof! in pops your Fairy Godmother. Sprinkle a little fairy dust, wave a wand, say a few magic words, and presto, you are a princess.

Heaven, however, requires a price that must be paid to enter in. It is reserved only for those who have labored to enter that place of rest, who have repented of their sins and asked Jesus Christ to save their souls, and who have then gone on to serve the Lord. Not everybody wants to do all that.

One other thing. Fairy Tales are just that – nice stories that sound good. Heaven <u>is</u> real and it <u>is</u> good.

Unfortunately, Hell is real also, and it isn't good. Don't get Fairy Tales and Heaven mixed up. We aren't going to get carried away to Heaven by wishful thinking, and it isn't going to happen just because we believe in magic. And it sure isn't going to happen for us unless we prepare for it. If we don't get right with God, it won't be the wicked witch that does us in; it will be the Devil that sinks his claws in us and drags us down to Hell.

Don't live your life in a fairy tale. If you want to walk on streets of gold someday, you have to travel the path of a Christian. That may not be as easy as making a wish, but it is the only way to make your dreams come true.

I Remember When We Were Young

I remember when we were young.

We were just kids, but we had answered the call from God to charge into battle. The whole idea of spiritual reality had just been opened up to us, and we knew for the first time that there really was a God, that there was a spiritual world all around us, and that there really was a Hell. We were willing to sacrifice our lives to the cause simply because it was the Truth.

It was more than just the fact that Jesus Christ was our Savior and that we had been changed from death unto life. We were able to see with distinct clarity that death was more real than life and that Judgment waited for every man. So, we shouldered the burden that God had given us and cast aside our futures to go into the battle to rescue lost souls from an eternity of torments.

I still remember those days of spiritual warfare. Fasts were never less than three days, and they were often. All-night prayer meetings were just exactly that – we prayed all night. We devoured the Word of God and made sure that young Christians made it to the reading groups to get tanked up. And then we took that fire and zeal to the streets and witnessed our hearts out for God.

I have no regrets. Sure, I could have a career right now, a fancy job, and plenty of money, but we gave our lives to the greatest cause of all time. In the end, the only things we really sacrificed were the unrealities of this life, and as a result, thousands of souls got saved.

I look back from a place of relative ease, but I still remember. I have a family now, a house, a car, and plenty of change in my pocket, but what I wouldn't give to go back to those exciting times of revival when scores of souls were coming in every day to get saved. Every day was a challenge to make ends meet, finances and comforts were scarce, and there was never enough time to take a break and relax. But oh, how charged we were! We were young, vibrant, and on fire for God.

The closer we get to that Final Day, the harder I pray for a restoration of the Body of Christ to that place of revival. I believe it will come. It may not come the way we expect, and it may not even come to our churches, but it will come.

And when it does, I want to be saddled up and ready to ride.

Brokenness

> *"...and he took the seven loaves, and gave thanks, and brake, and gave to his disciples to set before them..."*
> Mark 8:6

Is there such a thing as a painless sacrifice? Many of us know that there are mountaintops in the Lord and that there are also valleys. While we would rather bask in the sunshine on those mountaintops, we know that we only grow in the valleys. It is the way of Life.

Human nature will always opt for an easy way whenever possible. Why go looking for trouble? If we can accomplish the same things by avoiding pain or work, we will do it. Too often, we measure the value of a task not by its merits but by its price. If the price to accomplish something is too high, it's easier to let someone else pay it and hope to ride along in his or her wake.

But great miracles in God can only be accomplished through brokenness. The disciples could have run to the market to buy 7,000 loaves of bread, and it probably would have worked after a fashion, but it would have never filled their souls. Jesus broke the bread, and it filled the hungry. There is something in that broken, crucified walk that can take the mundane and bring forth Life. Nothing else will work.

In our desire to promote the Kingdom of God, have we chosen easy paths? Are we satisfied with results that work after a fashion? Are we looking for the blessings but not the sacrifice?

Great men in God are not born great; they are forged

in a furnace. They have a willingness to allow themselves to be broken so that the glory of God can be manifest in their lives. They have a focus not on themselves, their comfort, their own blessings, or their own lives, but on others.

A crucified walk in God leads only to the Cross. Jesus allowed his flesh, the Bread of Life, to be broken for us so that we may live. He calls us to that same path.

Simple solutions and carnal endeavors may work after a fashion. Prosperity, blessings, and ease may feed our bellies, but only brokenness will feed our souls.

Rain

"Ask ye of the Lord rain in the time of the latter rain...."
Zechariah 10:1

There are times when it can get pretty dry. I can remember times here in Texas when the air had a burnt feeling to it from lack of rain. 100 days of drought and no rain in sight. The grass was so dry, that it crunched under your feet. Cattle were being shipped out because they couldn't survive the drought, and people were dying from the heat.

In a time of spiritual drought, however, the stakes are higher. When souls perish, the price is an eternity in Hell.

The prophets all warn of a time just before the final coming of Jesus Christ when there would be a spiritual famine. Just as in His first coming when there were churches everywhere, there was no pasture for the flocks, and people were dying for the Truth. If what the prophets are saying is true, are we in that time right now?

As we see Jerusalem becoming a burdensome stone for the whole world, we look for the armies of the world to compass themselves around her. Although that has not quite happened just yet, we can clearly see the beginnings of that scenario unfold before us. We crossed a threshold on Sept. 11, 2001+ and the progression of events is rolling downhill to an ever-increasing crescendo. It's too late to go back. We are headed downhill.

How is it possible that with all the churches we see

around us, we could be in a spiritual drought? Are the prophets mistaken? Was that for some other time? Or have we just gotten so far away from God that we don't recognize the signs anymore?

Look down into the wells. Is there water flowing there? Are the wells of Salvation running through our streets? Are our altars filled with lost souls desperately seeking Salvation? Do we even have altar calls for the lost anymore? Are Christians broken at the altars crying out to God for an outpouring of the Spirit of God like we have seen in times past?

If the answer is no, then we are entering into those times of drought, and the prophets were right all along.

We may enjoy our weekly services, we may be enamored by our Tinseltown Televangelists, we may be deluged with offers to buy books and videos, go to conferences, sing songs, and wear T-shirts, but where are the souls? The Great Commission, the bottom line of Christianity, is to win lost souls.

There will be one last great revival, according to Joel, but it will come to those who answer the call that we see in chapter 2 of the Book of Joel. If you don't recognize the desperate need, you won't feel the call. If you are not grieved for the lost, there will be nothing to drive you to your knees in prevailing prayer. If you don't realize how dry it is right now, perhaps you have never known what it can be like when you are soaked by the Spirit of God pouring down from on high.

Pray for rain in this time of the latter rain. Just make sure you are inside the Ark when it does.

15 Minutes of Fame

What if you had 15 minutes of fame where you could say something to the entire world? What would you say? What is the message you want everyone to hear?

Would you tell them, "Jesus Christ is the Truth"?

Well, the ones who have experienced Salvation already know that, and those who have not been saved remain unconvinced. Is telling them again going to change their opinion or cause them to run out and get saved all of a sudden?

How about, "Love is the answer"?

We've gotten that message from everybody, from the Beatles to the Hippies to Martin Luther King. Has it changed anything? The songs are pretty, and it sounds so nice, but is the world now different because of it?

If you wanted to change the world, what would you say that would really affect a difference?

The fact is that most people have already formed their own opinions about Life and are going to believe what they want to believe. It will take something more than just words to turn their souls. People aren't going to just change their entire life just because you say so.

I believe that there is nothing more important than making sure your soul is right with God. How you spend your life on this side will determine where you spend Eternity on the other side. This side lasts a few years, and it's over. Eternity lasts forever. What could possibly be more important than making sure you escape Hell?

And yet, the world remains unconvinced.

Words, words, words. Debates and theological dissertations are, in and of themselves, just words. There has to be something more than just words to convince a human soul to come to a place of repentance and ask Jesus Christ to save them. There has to be power. And that power has to come from the Throne of God.

The Bible says that the Kingdom of God is not in word but in power. Not our power, but God's. In other words, if you ever want to win souls for Jesus Christ, then He must be the one speaking through your lips. If you are not speaking in the Spirit of God, you won't scare the fleas off a dog. Oh, but when the power of God is evident in your life, people will flock to you to hear the Truth because they can feel that you have the words of Life. There's just something about a real man or woman of God that is different. They've got power.

So, the question is not what you will say, but what will you <u>do</u> to get the power to preach in the power of the Holy Ghost? What are you willing to do to get to that place in God where you have the power to win souls?

Are you willing to pray your heart out to get to the Throne of God? Are you willing to read your face off to gain power from the Word of God? Are you willing to fast your guts out for lost souls? Yes, or no. There's your answer.

> *"And my speech and my preaching was not with enticing words of man's wisdom, but in demonstration of the Spirit and of power: that your faith should not stand in the wisdom of men, but in the power of God."*
> 1 Corinthians 2:4,5

Religious Spirit

In wandering through the middle of the Book of Matthew, I am struck with the disdain that Jesus had for the religious Pharisees of the time. He not only exhibited mere disdain, but he brought forth some serious condemnations. Neither was he alone, for he quoted heavily from the prophets.

One theme that Jesus struck upon over and over was their inability to see their own lack of Truth. Their eyes were covered with the trappings of their religious spirit, and not only could they not see, but they didn't want to see. And that was the sin that condemned them.

The Book, as Isaiah so eloquently puts it, is sealed unto them because they honor God with their lips, but their hearts are far from Him, and the real, chilling Fear of God is taught by rote (Isaiah 29:13). They can read it, but it is just text on paper – there is no anointing of the Spirit of God. They see it with their eyes, but their hearts desire something else.

So close. They hang onto that "form of godliness" so they can feel good about themselves without ever yielding to the humility of the Cross, but how few seek that lowly walk of the Nazarene. It seems so much better to eat off the Tree of the Knowledge of Good and Evil. But in the seeds of that fruit, we find Religion and that invisible sin of pride that blinds our eyes.

Why are they so blind and yet think that they can see?

You can't look with your eyes -- you'll only see the carnal. You can't rely on your own strength – you'll only go so far. You can't try to figure it out with your own carnal mind – you'll never understand the spiritual.

You have to surrender. You have to lean into the Spirit of the Lord instead of ecclesiastical foundations. You have to deny yourself and pick up the cross and follow Him.

Ah, there's the rub! No self-pride, no accomplishments or achievements, nothing worthy of ourselves. We have to drop everything that has to do with self. God gets all the glory – we get to serve.

That's the price that separates the religious from the saved, the carnal from the spiritual, and the sheep from the goats. It's all written in the Book.

It's just a matter of whether we want to see it.

The Death of Saul

> *Now the Philistines fought against Israel: and the men of Israel fled from before the Philistines, and fell down slain in mount Gilboa. 1Samuel 31:1*

After the battle, the men of Jabesh-Gilead recaptured the bodies of Saul and his sons, buried them, and fasted for seven days. I used to wonder why they went on a seven-day fast. After all, Saul was dead. What good was fasting for him going to do now? A little late, don't you think?

I have come to realize that their hearts were not cut for this carnal king that had been rejected by God but for Mount Zion, the people of God, and the future of the real church of God. The Philistines, the enemy of their souls, had crossed over Jordan, the bloodline of separation between the righteous and the unrighteous, and had conquered that which had been the territory of God. Israel, the church, had fallen.

Had they not been warned? Samuel the prophet had told Israel that, by choosing a carnal king instead of being led by God, they would succumb to the same things that all the other kingdoms of the world had fallen into. Saul, who had been anointed to be this new king over Israel, had fallen just like Samuel had said. What had once been the holy habitation of God had become carnal in nature and was no different than the other kingdoms of the world that God despised.

Saul had no armor to withstand the arrows of the enemy and fell down slain in Mount Gilboa. Our churches today, if they are not filled with the power of

God and led by His Spirit, will fall likewise. There is a difference between being led by the Spirit of God and being led by a carnal ecclesiastical structure that, although it looks and sounds like the real thing, has, somewhere along the line, fallen like Saul.

We will either become a Saul or a David – a carnal Christian or a spiritual Christian. Our churches also will be founded on the life-giving power that only comes from the Throne of God, or they will fall into a shell of what they used to be. Either you will choose to walk in the Spirit of God, or you will choose that comfortable, established, carnal church and fall down slain in Mount Gilboa.

Remember, there were two trees in the Garden of Eden – The Tree of Life and the Tree of Knowledge - the carnal knowledge of God. We choose one or the other.

About the Author

Dalen Garris has been in ministry since 1970 during the Jesus Movement in California. In 1997, he began a radio broadcast that ultimately spread to dozens of countries, including Israel and Saudi Arabia. His program, *Fire in the Hole*, was selected for broadcast four times a week across North America on the Sky Angel network as the Voice of Jerusalem.

A newspaper column followed, for which he has written over 700 articles, which were published in local newspapers and Christian magazines in several countries. He has also written several books and booklets.

Since 2004, he has been lighting the fires of revival in churches spread across sub-Saharan Africa. During the course of 16 years, he has preached in over 1,000 churches and has seen hundreds of churches set on fire and explode with growth. Hundreds of people have been supernaturally healed, and tens of thousands have been saved. And the fires are still burning.

Because of his work across Africa, Dalen Garris was awarded an honorary Doctorate in 2017 by the Northwestern Christian University of Florida.

Dr. Garris currently lives with Cindy, his wife of 45 years, in Waxahachie and is still heavily involved with churches across Africa. His pressing hope is in seeing this upcoming generation be the Gideon Generation that will usher in this last, great revival that he has preached about for so many years.

If you would like Dalen Garris to speak at your church or organization, please contact us for times and

THE EARLY YEARS

schedules.

Books by Dalen Garris:

Available at: **www.Revivalfre.org/books**

- Four Steps to Revival
- Do You Have Eternal Security?
- Standing in the Gap
- Two Covenants
- Fire in the Hole

Revival Campaigns

- The Kenya Diaries
- A Trumpet in Nigeria
- A Scent of Rain
- Into the Heart of Darkness
- Fire and Rain
- Revival Campaigns in Africa – 2019
- The Battle for Nigeria
- A Light in the Bush
- A Match in Dry Grass
- Planting a Seed in Liberia
- A Whisper in the Wind
- Talking With the Women, by Cindy

A Voice in the Wilderness series:

    vol. 1, The Journey Begins
    vol. 2, the Early Years
    vol. 3, Prophet Rising
    vol. 4, Revival in the Wings
    vol. 5, Sound of an Abundance of Rain
    vol. 6, Watchman, What of the Night?
    vol. 7, Mud and Heroes
    vol. 8, Ashes in the Morning
    vol. 9, Shaking the Olive Tree
    vol. 10, Winds of Change
    vol. 11, A Final Call

Booklets

*Available at: **www.Revivalfire.org/booklets/***

    A Volcano in Cape Verde
    Tanzania, 2011
    Nigeria, 2012
    Calvinism Critique
    When is the Rapture?

DALEN GARRIS

RevivalFire Ministries
PO Box 822
Waxahachie, TX 75168
dale@revivalfire.org

www.ingramcontent.com/pod-product-compliance
Lightning Source LLC
Chambersburg PA
CBHW031652040426
42453CB00006B/276